First Facts™

Materials

Paper

by Sara Louise Kras

Consultant:
Audrey Zink-Sharp, Associate Professor
Virginia Polytechnic Institute and State University
Department of Wood Science and Forest Products
Blacksburg, Virginia

Capstone
press
Mankato, Minnesota

First Facts is published by Capstone Press
151 Good Counsel Drive, P.O. Box 669, Mankato, Minnesota 56002
www.capstonepress.com

Library of Congress Cataloging-in-Publication Data
Kras, Sara Louise.
    Paper / by Sara Louise Kras.
    p. cm. — (First facts. Materials)
    Includes bibliographical references and index.
    Contents: Paper—What is paper?—Harvesting wood—From wood to paper—Many
kinds of paper—Portable paper—Strength of paper—Recycling paper—Amazing but
true!—Hands on.
    ISBN 0-7368-2513-4 (hardcover)
    1. Paper—Juvenile literature. 2. Papermaking—Juvenile literature. [1. Paper.] I. Title.
II. Series.
TS1105.5.K73 2004
676—dc22   2003015049

Editorial Credits

Heather Adamson and Blake A. Hoena, editors; Jennifer Bergstrom, series designer; Wanda
    Winch and Deirdre Barton, photo researchers; Gary Sundermeyer, photographer; Eric
    Kudalis, product planning editor

Photo Credits

Capstone Press/Gary Sundermeyer, cover, 1, 5, 6–7, 9, 12–13, 15, 19
Corbis/AFP, 20; Lester Lefkowitz, 11; Lindsay Hebberd, 16;
Index Stock Imagery/Steve Dunwell, 8
Photodisc/Siede Preis, 17

1 2 3 4 5 6 09 08 07 06 05 04

Table of Contents

Paper

Lora and her mom check their shopping list. Lora finds the carton of milk, the box of cereal, and the roll of paper towels. She gives the cashier coupons from the newspaper. She pays for the items with a $20 bill. Lora and her mom carry their groceries home in brown bags. Paper is all around us.

 Fun Fact:
Each year, the average American uses nearly 750 pounds (340 kilograms) of paper and paper products.

5

What Is Paper?

Paper is not a natural product. People make paper. Most paper is made from trees. The trees are cut into wood. Paper **mills** turn the wood into different kinds of paper.

 Fun Fact:
Only 17 percent of the wood gathered each year is used for making paper.

Harvesting Wood

Loggers cut down trees to **harvest** wood. New trees are planted to replace the old trees. This way, there are always enough trees to make paper.

People use wood from different trees to make different kinds of paper. Birch trees become thin paper like toilet paper. Pine trees are made into bags and boxes.

From Wood to Paper

In paper mills, machines chop wood into tiny chips. The wood chips are soaked in **chemicals** until they turn into a watery **pulp**. Another machine sprays the pulp onto a big screen. Hot rollers dry the pulp and flatten it into paper. The paper is then placed on large rolls.

 Fun Fact:
The water and chemicals leftover from making paper are used to make hundreds of other products, including plastic.

Many Kinds of Paper

Paper comes in many types. It can be thin like tissue paper. Or it can be thick like cardboard boxes.

Paper comes in many shapes and colors. Paper can be cut into flat sheets or folded into boxes. Paper can be **dyed** any color.

Portable Paper

Paper is light and easy to carry. Before paper, people sometimes wrote on stone. They also used heavy gold and silver coins for money. Books let people carry many pages of paper at once. Paper money folds easily into a pocket.

Hare ran and ran until he was sure he would

"This isn't even a race," he said to himself. "I thi

down and rest a bit. Then I'll finish and still h

of time to spare. There's no way that slowp

catch up with me!" So Hare lay down un

and soon fell fast asleep.

ould hear

running as

t when he saw

ot believe his eyes.

race. Hare could no

the finish line!

FINISH

Strength of Paper

Paper can be strong. People in Asia make colorful umbrellas out of paper. The umbrellas are strong enough to keep out rain.

Most packages are shipped in paper boxes. The sturdy cardboard costs less than shipping in wood or plastic crates.

Recycling Paper

Many types of paper can be **recycled**. Hot, soapy water washes ink off used paper. The wet paper turns into pulp. Often, a machine washes and bleaches the pulp to make it white. The pulp is then dried to make new paper. Recycling paper saves **energy** and trees.

Amazing But True!

Thousands of years ago, people in Egypt used papyrus plants as paper. Papyrus stalks grew along the Nile River. People cut the papyrus into strips. They pounded and soaked the strips before weaving them together. Once dried, the papyrus sheets were used for writing and drawing.

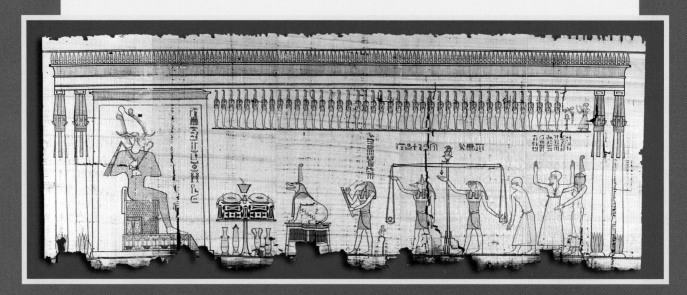

Hands On: Make Recycled Paper

Strong wood fibers allow paper to be recycled several times. Have an adult help you make your own recycled paper.

What You Need

2 or 3 pages of newspaper torn in pieces
large dishtub
water
small piece of screen
open-faced cookie cutter

hand mixer
small cup
plastic bag
2 sheets of felt
rolling pin

What You Do

1. Put a handful of newspaper pieces into the tub. Cover the pieces with water. Let the pieces soak until they are soft.
2. Use the mixer to stir the pieces until they break apart.
3. Have an adult hold the screen over the tub. Place the cookie cutter on the screen.
4. Use the cup to scoop the mixture into the cutter. Press the pulp down with your fingers to form a flat layer inside the cutter.
5. Remove the cutter and flip the screen onto the plastic bag.
6. Peel the paper from the bag and place it between two sheets of felt. Gently use a rolling pin to squeeze out any extra water. Allow to dry for several hours. Then remove the felt and use your paper.

Glossary

chemical (KEM-uh-kuhl)—a substance that creates a reaction; chemicals react with wood so that it falls apart and turns into pulp.

dye (DYE)—to change something's color by adding chemicals

energy (EN-ur-jee)—power, such as electricity

harvest (HAR-vist)—to collect or gather; loggers harvest trees for wood.

mill (MIL)—a building with machinery for turning raw materials into products

pulp (PUHLP)—a soft, wet mixture

recycle (ree-SYE-kuhl)—to make used items into new products

Read More

Llewellyn, Claire. *Paper*. Material World. New York: Franklin Watts, 2002.

Marshall, Pam. *From Tree to Paper.* Start to Finish. Minneapolis: Lerner Publications Co., 2003.

Internet Sites

FactHound offers a safe, fun way to find Internet sites related to this book. All of the sites on FactHound have been researched by our staff.

Here's how:
1. Visit *www.facthound.com*
2. Type in this special code **0736825134** for age-appropriate sites. Or enter a search word related to this book for a more general search.
3. Click on the Fetch It button.

FactHound will fetch the best sites for you!

Index